DECORATIVE STAMPING
for the home

MICHELLE POWELL

SEARCH PRESS

First published in Great Britain 1998

Search Press Limited
Wellwood, North Farm Road,
Tunbridge Wells, Kent TN2 3DR

ISBN 0 85532 877 0

Suppliers
If you have any difficulty in obtaining any of the materials and equipment mentioned in this book, then please write to the publishers for a current list of stockists, which includes firms who operate a mail-order service:
Search Press Limited, Wellwood,
North Farm Road, Tunbridge Wells,
Kent TN2 3DR, England

Publishers' note
All the step-by-step photographs in this book feature the author, Michelle Powell, demonstrating the technique of decorative stamping. No models have been used.

Colour separation by P&W Graphics, Singapore
Printed in Spain by Elkar S. Coop. Bilbao 48012

I would like to thank all the team at Rubber Stampede, especially Wendy and Anna for their amazing artistic help and continual support, Barrie for his wood working expertise, Roger for doing the hardest job of all – the spell checking – and finally Sam and all the US team. Thanks to Mandy and Nicki for the loan of props and homes.

A big thank you also to everyone involved at Search Press – Roz, Chantal, Lotti and Julie to name but a few.

And of course, special thanks to Jon for putting up with everything I care to throw at him, all my daft ideas . . . and for smiling throughout.

*The biggest thanks go to Mum and Dad and Nan and Gramp. This book is dedicated to them
. . . even though they do not expect it.*

The publishers would like to thank Crowson Fabrics Ltd., Bellbrook Park, Uckfield, East Sussex, TN22 1QZ for supplying the fabric which is used as the basis for the homemade stamp featured on pages 10–11.

Contents

INTRODUCTION

About this book • *Materials* • *Making a stamp*
Basic Techniques • *Creative stamping* • *Arranging a design*

Stamping has come a long way since the humble potato print, and decorative stamping is fast becoming a key home decoration technique – it is quick, simple, effective and fun. Armed with a stamp, some paint and a little imagination, you can transform your home in just a few hours. The technique is so straightforward that skills can be mastered by everyone, regardless of artistic ability.

Fashions change rapidly in home decoration and soon a room can look out-of-date. Stamping is the inexpensive solution. This book shows you how to create a truly unique and original home by stamping everything from the smallest flower pot to an entire room. All the basic techniques are covered, including choosing a stamp, making a stamp, applying the paint and arranging the design.

With the right stamp and paint, decorative stamping is an extremely versatile technique and even curved or uneven surfaces can be stamped. Increased development in paint technology, means that virtually any surface can now be decorated, and the following pages explore just some of the different surfaces that can be stamped. Smooth, slightly porous surfaces are the easiest to stamp – wooden furniture, plastered walls, card and paper are all ideal – but fabric is also easily transformed. A dazzling array of effects can even be achieved on non-porous surfaces such as glass, glazed ceramics and mirrors.

A multitude of stamps designed for different purposes, are now readily available from craft, gift and DIY stores. Even the most basic stamp can produce amazing results – by altering the colour and arrangement, you can produce endless possibilities. Stamps can be used on a large scale to add patterns and stylish borders to walls, or they can be applied sparingly to create simple decorative details for a room.

Although many techniques and projects are featured in this book, they are merely a catalyst to inform, inspire and help you on your way. The best results will often come quite by accident, so experiment, be creative and have fun. Whether you want to cheer up old furniture, introduce new colour to plain curtains or add a designer touch to your paintwork – let your imagination run wild. You will be astonished at the effects you can achieve.

Materials

In order to create a basic stamped impression, the only materials needed are a stamp, some paint and an applicator sponge. Many paints can be used with decorative stamps, each giving a different effect. Throughout this book, unless otherwise stated, I have used a multipurpose decorative stamping paint that is suitable for stamping any surface, including fabric. It is water-soluble, permanent, acrylic-based and fully opaque.

Stamps

Traditional pictorial rubber stamps have been popular for many years, and these are used for crafting greetings cards and stationery; they are available in many different designs, from elegant images to cute cartoon characters.

Recently, new ranges of stamps designed for a multitude of purposes, have come on the market. Different results can be achieved with each type. Large stamps, with foam, polystyrene or flock surfaces are aimed specifically at creating home decor effects. As foam is slightly porous, it will hold plenty of paint, giving a clear and true stamped impression, especially on wood, walls and fabrics.

The key to choosing a good stamp for decorative stamping is to select one the correct size. If you are embarking on a home decoration project and you have a relatively large area to cover, your stamped image will need to be at least 4cm (1½in) square, preferably even larger (although this will vary depending on purpose and taste). A stamp without fussy detail may render a more pleasing finish.

Try holding the stamp in your hand to check for fit and ease of control. A stamp mounted on a soft foam backing is more forgiving than one with a wooden handle. The foam will bend around curved surfaces and can be pressed into uneven walls.

Other materials

The materials listed here and on pages 8–9 are required for the various techniques in this book. Most are everyday items that you probably already have. More specialist items are available from craft, home decor and DIY stores.

1. **Paintbrushes** I use a selection, including large decorator's brushes for backgrounds, and small paintbrushes for detailing.
2. **Wedge applicator sponges** Used to apply paint to and blend colours on a stamp.
3. **Plate** This is used as a palette.
4. **Various decorative stamping paints** Used for stamping, and for adding detail.
5. **Emulsion paint** This is used for basecoating, or painting walls and small furniture.
6. **Wallpaper paste** This can be mixed with paint to make it more translucent and to increase the open drying time, which is useful when stamping off. Glycerine can be used instead.
7. **Glycerine** This can be mixed with paint to add translucency, and increase open drying time.
8. **Air-hardening clay** You can press a stamp into soft clay to create an embossed pattern.
9. **Craft knife** For cutting clay.
10. **Nailbrush** For cleaning stamps.
11. **Damp cloth** Useful in case of mistakes, and for wiping up spillages.
12. **Soft cloth** For applying and buffing up wax.
13. **Scrap paper** You can create large masks from this. A pile of scrap paper should also be placed under thin fabric when stamping.
14. **Sticky notelets** These can be used to create small masks.
15. **Ruler** Used for measuring and cutting against.
16. **Cutting mat** For working on when using a scalpel.
17. **Dutch metal leaf** Used to gild.

18. **Gilding size** For attaching Dutch metal leaf.

19. **Soft brush** For brushing off excess metal leaf.

20. **Cotton buds** For applying dots of paint.

21. **Tailor's chalk** For marking fabric.

22. **Scalpel** For cutting out paper masks, foam for a stamp, and for other precision cutting.

23. **Pencil** For general use, including marking out a design.

24. **Tracing paper** Used to trace an image when making a stamp.

25. **MDF block** Medium-density fibreboard is used as a backing for a homemade stamp.

26. **High-density foam** Used to make a stamp.

27. **Wood dowel** A square of foam can be glued to the end of dowelling to make a small stamp.

28. **Glitter and glue pen** Used to add decoration to stamped images.

29. **Glue** An adhesive stick is used to adhere tracing paper to foam when making a stamp. Solvent glue is for general use.

30. **Iron** For fixing stamped fabric.

31. **Masking tape** Both normal and low-tack tape are used (depending on the surface) for masking off areas from paint.

32. **Water sprayer** For dampening a stamp when working on velvet (see page 36).

33. **Furniture wax** Used to protect a wooden stamped piece. If tinted, it can be used to colour.

34. **Gilding wax (gold and copper)** This can be rubbed in to create a subtle metallic effect.

35. **Tile varnish** This protects the painted or stamped images by sealing the surface.

36. **Water-based varnish** Used for varnish stamping, frosted stamping and for sealing.

Making a stamp

You can custom-make stamps from a number of different materials. I find the best results are achieved using high-density foam, as detailed images can be easily cut out. I have used a piece of MDF (medium density fibreboard) for the stamp handle, but any wood will do as long as it is thick enough to hold comfortably.

Inspiration for stamp designs can come from many sources – wallpaper, fabric and greetings cards, for example, or you can use your own artwork. In this demonstration I have taken a flower motif from curtain fabric.

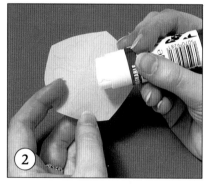
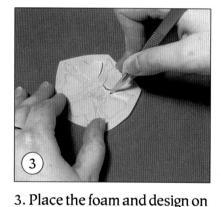

Note
Always use a very sharp scalpel when cutting high-density foam in order to get a clean cut.

1. Place a piece of tracing paper over your chosen design and go around the outline with a pencil.

2. Cut very roughly around the outside of the design. Use an adhesive stick to add a little glue to the back of the tracing paper then press it on to a piece of thin high-density foam.

3. Place the foam and design on a cutting mat, and cut around the shapes of the design using a scalpel. Work slowly and carefully and try to keep the blade as upright as possible as you work.

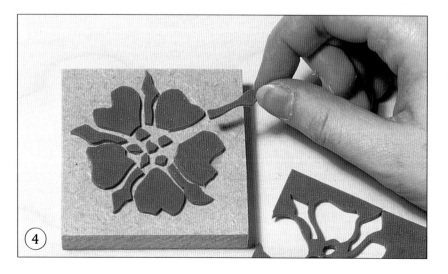

4. Arrange the foam pieces on a small block of MDF or wood. Use solvent glue to stick the foam pieces down.

OPPOSITE
This coordinating lampshade and border are stamped with homemade stamps inspired by curtain fabric. Two stamps are cut out – a flower and a leaf – and they are alternated to create a simple but effective design.

Basic techniques

There are many methods of creating an image with a stamp. For most decorative effects, paint is used rather than an ink pad. The paint can be applied in a number of ways, including with a paintbrush, a wedge applicator sponge or a sponge roller. A wedge applicator sponge is the most versatile tool for applying paint. It is quick and easy to use and gives an even covering of paint to the correct thickness. This method also allows any number of colours to be applied to one stamp to create stunning multicoloured impressions and soft, subtle colour blending.

Note

If you make a mistake, wipe away the stamped image using a clean damp cloth. Wash the stamp, reapply the paint and start again!

You can touch up an image using a small paintbrush.

1. Decant pools of paint on to a palette. Press a wedge applicator sponge into your first colour.

2. Press the paint into the sponge using the side of the palette, then dab the sponge on to the stamp.

3. Apply a second colour using a clean applicator sponge. Turn the sponge round and use a clean corner to blot over the line and blend the colours together.

4. Apply additional colours. Press the stamp firmly on to your surface. Press each area of the stamp down evenly.

5. Hold your surface still and then lift the stamp straight up, without tilting it or shifting the position.

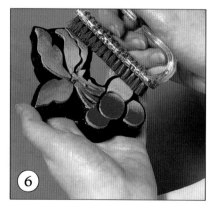

6. Place the stamp in a basin of water or under a tap. Scrub gently with a soft nailbrush to clean the stamp. Leave to dry.

Different results can be achieved with a single stamp by simply varying the colour combination.

Creative stamping

Varied and exciting effects are easy to achieve using varnishes, glazes and gilding size rather than paint for stamping. Try experimenting with other materials to create techniques of your own.

Stamping with varnish

This technique uses varnish to act as a resist. The following demonstration is worked using a clear, water-based satin varnish, but you could use any clear varnish. This technique works best on smooth surfaces, particularly wood.

1. Apply clear varnish to the stamp using an applicator sponge, then press onto your surface. Leave until fully dry.

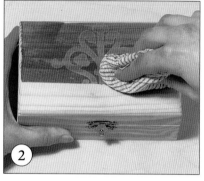

2. Mix one part paint to one part water to create a colourwash. Dab a clean cloth into the paint mixture and then wipe over the surface and over the varnished image. Leave to dry.

Playing card box
A subtle effect can be created using a simple varnish-stamped motif. A wash of paint is applied to highlight the image and bring out the natural grain of the wood.

Stamping off

This technique uses the stamp to remove paint, and it is achieved with two colours. You can use dark on light or light on dark. You get a subtler effect if you use two shades of the same colour, as shown here. The stamping off technique is only effective if you work quickly as the topcoat can only be stamped off while it is still wet.

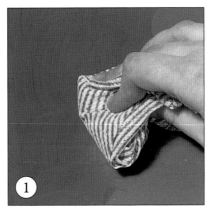

Note
When stamping off, mix wallpaper paste or glycerine into the paint to give it a longer open drying time.

1. Apply a basecoat of paint then leave to dry. Mix up a second colour mixture using one part paint to three parts ready-mixed wallpaper paste. Dip a cloth into this mixture and then wipe over the basecoat in random swirling strokes.

2. Press a clean dry stamp on to the painted surface and then remove it. If you are stamping off lots of images, repeat, working quickly so as not to allow the topcoat to dry.

Place mat
Create a stylish place mat by stamping off a darker top coat of paint to reveal a lighter base coat colour.

Frosted stamping

This is a very effective decorative technique which uses varnish mixed with white paint, to produce a frosted glass effect. It is a good idea to apply a coat of clear acrylic varnish to protect your finished piece.

1. Decant one part clear water-based varnish and one part white paint on to a clean palette. Mix together thoroughly.

2. Apply the paint mixture to the stamp, and then press the stamp lightly on to a glass surface, taking great care not to let the stamp slide. Leave to dry.

Glass vase
Transform a plain vase quickly and simply by using a translucent mix of paint and varnish to stamp a frosted image.

16

Gilding

You can apply gilding size to a stamp and use it to create brilliant metallic gilded images. The size acts like glue, so when the Dutch metal leaf is applied, it adheres only to the stamped image.

1. Apply size to a stamp and then stamp on to your surface. Leave to dry for approximately five minutes, until the size goes clear but still feels tacky.

2. Place a sheet of Dutch metal leaf over the stamped size. Press the leaf on to the size by tapping it lightly with a soft, clean, dry paintbrush. Use the same brush to brush off the leaf and reveal the gilded image.

Candlestick
Add elegance to your stamping by creating gilded images using size and Dutch metal leaf.

Note
Clean the stamp immediately after use with warm water and a soft nailbrush. Never allow size to dry on a stamp.

17

Arranging a design

Stamping is a fascinating technique, with huge potential. Initially, it may be difficult to see how a single stamped image can be used to create a whole interior scheme. However, just by altering the colour used on a stamp you can create a different look. With multiple stamped images, endless permutations of design and layout are possible. Stamp images in rows to create stripes, up and down for zig-zags, randomly all over, or in small clusters. Once started, you will soon find that more and more ideas will flow.

Certain images lend themselves better to certain designs. Look at the outer shape of the stamp. One that is basically square or rectangular will be best suited for rigid stripe or border designs. A stamp with a very irregular outline can create interesting random or cluster patterns.

Some stamps have a definite right way up – bear this in mind when stamping, but remember that you can still deploy a certain amount of artistic license. There are no rules in stamping; if you think an image looks effective stamped upside down, then stamp it that way!

If you are unsure of your chosen design, stamp several images on scrap paper before you begin your project. Cut out the images roughly, then move them around until you are happy with the design.

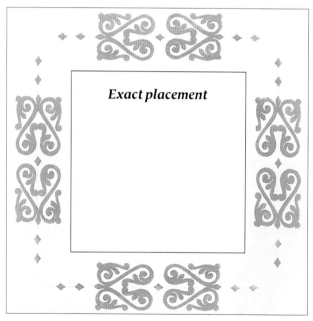

Some projects require exact placement of stamped images. For this design, the image is stamped several times on to acetate and a cross is drawn in the centre of each image. A cross is then drawn on the back of the stamp, in exactly the same place. The acetate images are moved around on the surface to find the best positioning for the design. The crosses are transferred from the acetate sheet to the stamping surface. The crosses on the surface are then lined up with the cross on the stamp for perfect positioning.

This design is worked by ruling two lines on the surface, with the gap in between, the approximate size of the stamp. The stamps are then applied between these lines and are spaced by eye. If working on a small object, start by stamping one image in the centre then fill in either side. Try alternating two or three different images or creating multiple rows of stamped images. If exact positioning is required, cut a strip of card the width of the desired gap and use this as a spacer between the stamps.

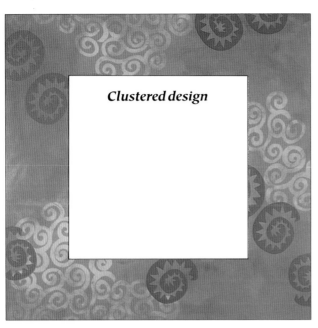

Clustered design

Random design

This design is stamped by varying the position of the image and then over-stamping with a second image. A cluster of stamped images is ideal for decorating small irregular-shaped spaces. Try to avoid filling all the available space.

This design is stamped randomly, varying the position of each stamp. Spacing is important: on smaller projects, the stamped images need to be quite close together; if stamping a large wall, the images can afford to be spaced 0.5–1m (2–3ft) apart.

Structured all-over design

Naturalistic arrangement

Checks, diamonds, stripes and zig-zags are all structured patterns, where exact positioning is needed. Pencil lines are ruled to indicate the central position of the stamped image on the surface. The centre top and centre bottom are marked on the back of the stamp, and the dots are then matched up with the pencil lines.

This trompe l'oeil effect is created by positioning the stamped images by eye, in natural-looking clusters. The images in the foreground are masked and further images are then stamped in the background several times without reapplying paint, so that they begin to get more faint.

19

WOOD, PLASTER, PAPER AND CARD

Gilded writing slope • Floral hat box • Gothic mirror
Children's toy box

Paper is the obvious material to start stamping on. It is cheap, easy to use and readily available. For any project, I would recommend practising first on scrap paper to get used to the feel of the stamp and to experiment with colour combinations. Any paper or card that has a smooth surface is excellent for stamping on, and no special technique is needed. Textured paper or card can also be used, but you should stamp carefully to ensure the image is crisp. There are many beautiful handmade papers available and these can be stamped to create luxurious writing paper, gift wrap and greetings cards. Paper is also the ideal medium to cover other items with, as you can stamp on the paper whilst it is flat, and then glue it to a three-dimensional object – a notebook, storage box or small piece of furniture, for example.

Wood is also an ideal stamping surface. You can stamp on to any real wood whether it is untreated, varnished, waxed or painted. Ensure the wood is clean and free from dust before you begin. If you are stamping on to untreated wood, sand it to a reasonably smooth finish first. Take care when stamping wooden surfaces covered with gloss paint or varnish, as the stamp may slide. Protect a finished wooden piece by applying a couple of coats of any clear matt, satin or gloss varnish.

Stamping is also perfect for plastered walls, particularly those painted with emulsion. Before stamping, clean the walls with a damp cloth to ensure that they are grease- and dust-free. If you are stamping on to newly-painted walls, make sure you wait until they are fully dry. As you are stamping on to a vertical rather than a horizontal surface, you must remember to press evenly all over the back of the stamp to ensure a clear image. When stamping a whole room, start at the top and work down the wall so that you do not smudge the images you have just stamped.

Gilded writing slope

The changing shapes and colours of autumnal leaves inspired the design for this pine writing slope. The slope is first stained using instant coffee to give a very rich, natural look, and it is finished with clear wax which produces a subtle, warm sheen. Three gilded leaf images add a sophisticated touch, making this writing slope ideal for the home, office or study.

You will need
Writing slope
Medium grade sandpaper
Damp cloth
Boiling water
Instant coffee
Cup and teaspoon
6.5cm (2½in) paintbrush
Small paintbrush
Decorative stamping paint:
  green, terracotta, brown,
  red, yellow and black
Decorative stamps: two
  different leaves
Gold Dutch metal leaf
Gilding size
Clean, soft, dry brush
Clear furniture wax
Clean, soft cloth
Glycerine
Applicator sponges and palette
Low-tack masking tape
Pencil and ruler

1. Prepare the wooden surface by lightly sanding all over using medium grade sandpaper. Wipe with a damp cloth to remove all traces of dust.

2. Add four heaped teaspoons of instant coffee to half a cup of boiling water. Paint this over the slope to achieve a rustic effect. Leave to dry. Apply a second coat to strengthen the colour.

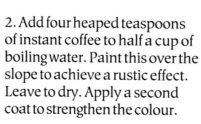

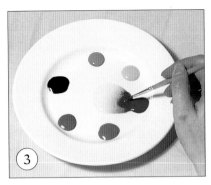

3. Transfer pools of green, terracotta, brown, red, yellow and black paint on to a palette. For each colour, mix approximately one part paint to one part glycerine – this will give a translucent finish to the paints.

4. Apply green, brown and yellow to one of the leaf stamps using an applicator sponge. Blend the colours on the stamp (see page 12). Stamp a random pattern over the desk lid. Repeat with the second leaf stamp to fill in the spaces, using terracotta, red, brown, black and yellow. Leave to dry.

5. Mark three 9cm (3½in) squares down the left-hand side of the lid, 2cm (¾in) from the edge. On the top, mark five thin stripes, approximately 9 x 0.5cm (3½ x ¼in). Use lengths of low-tack masking tape to mask the surrounding area and between the stripes.

6. Load a 6.5cm (2½in) brush with black, brown and red paint and use this to stipple over the squares on the lid, and the stripes on the top (see step 4, page 61). Leave to dry. Remove the masking tape.

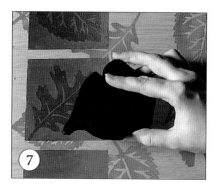

7. Apply gilding size to the stamp using a sponge applicator (see page 17) and stamp centrally on to the brown squares. Leave the size to dry for about five minutes, until it goes clear, but is just tacky.

8. Lay gold metal leaf over the size and tap down with a clean, soft, dry brush (see page 17). Brush away any excess gold leaf. Use these scraps to fill in any small gaps. Leave to dry overnight.

Note
If you rub the bristles of a clean, dry paintbrush over your hair, you will create static. You can use this static to pick up scraps of gold leaf.

9. Rub over the entire writing slope using clear furniture wax and a soft cloth. This will seal the colours and create a hardwearing finish.

OPPOSITE
Gilded writing slope
This writing slope features gilded leaf motifs and blended multicoloured stamping. It is easy to create a great variety of matching writing paper and desk accessories. Here I have stamped the leaf on to small squares of paper, combined these with roughly gilded squares and squares of handmade paper and then glued them into position on an ink bottle and note book. The fabric on the noticeboard is also decorated using the leaf stamps.

Floral hat box

This pretty floral stamped box creates stylish storage and is perfect for organising treasured possessions. The box I have used is approximately 15cm (6in) tall, with a diameter of 27cm (10½in). If your box is a different size, then you will need to adjust the length of muslin needed; this should be approximately three-and-a-half times the diameter of the box. The hat box I have used has eyelet holes for threading the cord handle. If your box does not have holes, these can be easily made using a bradawl or eyelet pliers. Alternatively, you can omit the handle.

You will need

Hat box, 27cm (10½in) in diameter, 15cm (6in) high

Emulsion paint: lilac

2.5cm (1in) paintbrush

Small paintbrush

Decorative stamping paint: purple, lavender, mid-green, jade, dusty pink, pale pink and white

Decorative stamps: daisy, anemone, leaves

Applicator sponges and palette

Cotton buds

Pencil and ruler

Purple muslin, 15 x 80cm (6 x 31½in)

Thin purple cord, 65cm (26in)

Scrap paper

Sticky notelets

Solvent glue

Scalpel and cutting mat

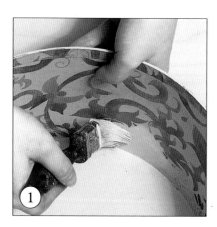

1. Apply a coat of lilac emulsion to the inside and outside of the hat box, and the inside and outside of the lid. Leave to dry before applying another coat. Leave to dry.

2. Blend purple and lavender on the daisy stamp (see page 12). Stamp at equal intervals around the box, leaving enough space in between each image for the anemone stamp. Leave to dry.

3. Blend pale pink, dusty pink and lavender on the anemone stamp and then use this to stamp in between the daisies. Leave to dry.

4. Stamp the daisy on to a sticky notelet. Leave to dry before cutting around the outline of the shape using a scalpel; this will create a mask. Repeat with the anemone stamp.

Note

You may find it easier to make several masks of each flower for this project. To do this, peel off a few sticky notelets together, stamp on to the top one and then cut through all the layers at once.

If you want to make reusable masks, stamp the images on to acetate then cut them out. Use a re-positionable spray adhesive to lightly coat the back of the masks each time you want to use them. Clean with water after use.

5. Position the masks directly over the stamped images. Blend mid-green and jade on the leaf stamp and then stamp between the flowers. Repeat all around the box, then remove the masks and leave to dry.

6. Dip the end of a cotton bud into white paint and use this to create small clusters of dots at the edges of the flowers to represent gypsophila.

7. Divide the lid into an equal number of sections. To do this, wrap a long strip of scrap paper around the circumference of the lid. Trim the ends where they meet. Fold the strip in half, then in half again and continue folding until the paper is the width you would like the stripe on the lid. Unfold the paper and wrap it around the box. Use a pencil to mark the lid at each paper fold.

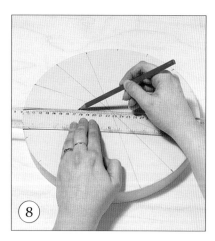

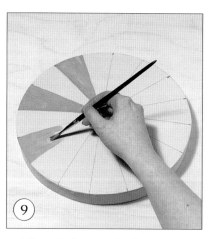

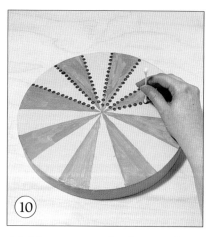

8. Join up the pencil marks on the lid to make stripes. Try to leave only very faint pencil lines.

9. Mix a little purple decorative stamping paint with lavender. Use a small paintbrush to paint every other stripe. Do not worry if the edges of the stripes are not very neat. Leave to dry.

10. Use a cotton bud to apply an evenly spaced row of purple dots along the edges of the stripes. Leave to dry.

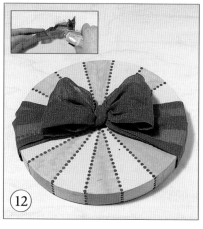

11. Form two loops in the centre of the length of purple muslin (a). Cross one of the loops over the other (b) and then bring the crossed-over loop up through the hole (c). Arrange the fabric to form a bow (d).

12. Use solvent glue to attach each end of the muslin fabric inside the rim of the lid.

13. Thread purple cord through the holes in the side of the hat box to make a handle. Knot the cord on the inside to secure it.

OPPOSITE
Floral hat boxes
These stamped flowers are masked and then the background between is filled in with leaves. When the masks are removed, the leaves appear to be behind the flowers. Floral stamps lend themselves particularly well to being grouped to make long swags or wreaths, as shown by the fire screen. You can alter the shades of the flowers to match an existing colour scheme, or use the technique to add small decorative details to existing furniture.

Gothic mirror

For this project, I have used a very unusual mirror. Look for something similar in junk shops, or approach a local carpenter to make one specially for you. Whatever mirror you choose to decorate, you can adapt this technique to suit.

Before you start, you will need to hand cut the key and Tudor stamps using the patterns provided. Trace off the images and follow the instructions given on page 10. Alternatively, you could use a pre-cut stamp of your choice.

You will need
Mirror frame
MDF block
High-density foam
Scalpel
Cutting mat
Tracing paper
Pencil
Adhesive stick
Solvent glue
Emulsion paint: yellow and
  dark yellow
Decorative stamping paint:
  mid-green, dark green,
  brown, red and dark yellow
Applicator sponges and palette
Wallpaper paste
Sand or sawdust
Powdered filler
5cm (2in) paintbrush
1cm (½in) paintbrush
Clear acrylic matt varnish

*Full-size patterns for the
Tudor and Key stamps*

1. Remove the mirror glass and doors. Lightly sand if necessary. Mix one part sand (or sawdust) with one part yellow emulsion and one part powdered filler. Add one part water if the mixture is too dry.

2. Stipple a coat of this mixture on to the mirror frame and doors. Leave to dry.

3. Mix a wash using three parts wallpaper paste to one part dark yellow emulsion paint and apply this to the frame. Press the clean key stamp onto the wet paint using the stamping off technique to create a subtle pattern (see page 15).

4. Apply dark green, mid-green, dark yellow, red, dark pink and brown paint to the Tudor stamp. Stamp the image on the inside of one of the door panels, so that the bottom of the stamp roughly lines up with the centre. Load the stamp with paint again, turn it upside down then line it up with the bottom of the first stamp. Repeat on the other door.

5. Mix one part red paint with one part dark pink paint, one part sand (or sawdust) and one part powdered filler. Stipple this mixture over the wooden decorative trim, the coving and the moulding on the frame using a 1cm (½in) brush. Reattach the mirror glass and doors to the frame. Finish with a coat of clear acrylic matt varnish, applied in a stippling action to add to the aged, rustic look.

Gothic mirror

Reminiscent of times gone by, this Gothic styled mirror makes a stunning centrepiece for any room and the plant pot complements it perfectly. Two different stamping techniques are used, stamping off and stamping on, to give a rich layered effect. The key and Tudor stamps used are hand-cut from thin, high-density foam.

Children's toy box

You can decorate a toy chest with a patchwork of pastel shapes and patterns. Pearlescent paint is used throughout this project to create a soft shimmer to the stamping. The pearlescent paint is made by mixing equal parts of coloured paint with silver paint. Glitter is added for extra sparkle, and dimensional outlining paste is used to create the effect of stitching between the different stamped patches. Masking tape is used to section off each area, making it easy to combine many different colours and patterns on one box. The same technique can be used to create a matching lid.

1. Paint the chest with white emulsion paint. Leave to dry then apply a second coat. Leave to dry. Use a pencil and ruler to mark random patchwork squares all over the box. The sizes and shapes do not matter, as long as they are large enough to allow room for the stamped images.

2. Mask some of the areas off with masking tape. Mix one part lavender paint with one part silver paint and two parts ready-mixed wallpaper paste. Use a rag to move this paint mixture around within the masked shapes to create an uneven finish. Leave to dry.

3. Mix one part lavender paint to one part silver paint to give a pearlescent effect. Stamp swirls within some of the lilac shapes, and leave others unstamped.

33

4. Remove the masking tape and repeat steps 2 and 3 with other colours and the leaf and flower stamps. Change stamps and colours randomly. Leave to dry. Continue until the box is covered.

5. Stamp bugs on to some of the squares, using colours of your choice. Blend the colours on the stamp before stamping (see page 12). Leave to dry.

6. Apply glue to the spots on the bugs' wings, the antennae, and the central wing lines. Sprinkle with glitter then leave to dry.

7. Use dimensional outlining paste to draw small lines and crosses around the edges of the shapes; this will represent patchwork stitching. Leave to dry. Apply a coat of clear matt acrylic varnish.

Children's toy box
Pearlescent pastel colours give this toy box a whimsical quality, making it ideal for a young child's room. The patchwork effect is created by masking separate areas, stamping, then adding stitch detailing with outlining paste. Small pictures are stamped to match.

FABRICS

Eastern clothes screen • Ethnic throw

Decorative stamping is an ideal way to decorate plain fabric, perhaps to match with an existing scheme or to jazz up older furnishings. Most fabrics can be stamped successfully, but cotton or cotton-mix fabrics with a fine, close weave are ideal. Using the correct paint is crucial if you want your stamped images to be washable. Multi-purpose stamping paints suitable for use on fabrics are available, as well as paints designed specifically for use on fabric. Follow the manufacturer's instructions carefully for best results.

Wash, dry and iron all fabrics before stamping, to remove any dirt and the manufacturer's dressing. Paint will seep through fabric when you are stamping, so it is best to work on a flat surface, protected with scrap paper or several layers of old sheeting. Heavy or thick fabrics may need an extra thick layer of paint in order to achieve even coverage. If this is the case, apply the paint to the stamp using a paintbrush, rather than an applicator sponge. Try not to move the fabric while you are stamping, as the wet paint that seeps on to the backing paper or sheeting may mark the underside of the fabric. When the paint is dry, you should iron on the reverse side of the fabric to fix the paint; set the iron at a temperature suitable for the fabric you are working on.

The only fabrics that are difficult to stamp are those with a very large weave or slub. Some 100% synthetic fabrics will not take the paint very well. For practicality, any fabric that you cannot iron is unsuitable as you are unable to fix the paints. To clean stamped items, use a cool wash, or hand wash them. All home-use fabric paints will start to fade after repeated washing.

Note

It is possible to stamp on velvet, without using paint! Spray the clean stamp with a water sprayer. Place the velvet on top of the stamp, plush side down, facing the front of the image. Press the velvet above the stamp using an iron on a medium setting. Hold the iron in place for two seconds, then lift up for a moment before pressing it down again for one second. The pile of the velvet will depress in the shape of the stamp to leave a subtle image, that will catch the light.

Eastern clothes screen

Replace old or worn-out fabric on a screen with delicate stamped muslin panels. I have worked three panels – two in rust and one in cream, but you could work other combinations. When stamping on fabric such as muslin, remember to protect your work surface with layers of paper or old sheeting, as the paint will go straight through.

I have not given specific fabric sizes for this project as all screens will vary. Before you begin, remove any fabric from the existing screen, and use this as a template for cutting the new fabric panels; remember to leave a 2cm (¾in) seam allowance on all sides. Wash, dry and iron the new fabric.

You will need
Iron or wooden screen frame

Cream muslin: two 15cm (6in) squares, one 8cm (3¼in) square, one panel piece

Rust muslin: one 15cm (6in) square, two 8cm (3¼in) squares, two panel pieces

Gold organza: three 11cm (4¼in) squares

4m (4yd) rust ribbon and 2m (2yd) cream ribbon

Scrap paper or old sheeting

Rust and cream sewing thread

Decorative stamping paint: rust, gold and cream

Decorative stamp: wrought iron shape

Applicator sponges and palette

Pins

Scissors

Iron

1. Lay one of the muslin panel pieces out on a smooth flat surface, on top of a layer of paper or old sheeting. Apply gold paint to your stamp then stamp a row of images down the centre of the panel, beginning approximately 38cm (15in) from the top. Try to hold the fabric flat as you stamp.

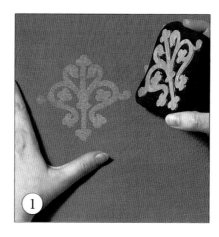

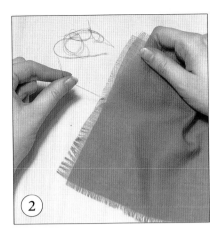

2. Remove threads from the edges of each fabric square to create a 3mm (⅛in) frayed edge.

3. Apply rust paint to the stamp then stamp one image in each of the four corners of the large rust squares. Now stamp cream images on the large cream fabric squares.

5. Arrange the squares on top of each other with the smallest on top, and the gold organza in the middle.

4. Apply rust paint to the stamp then stamp one image in the centre of each of the small cream squares. Now stamp cream images on the small rust fabric squares. Leave the gold organza un-stamped.

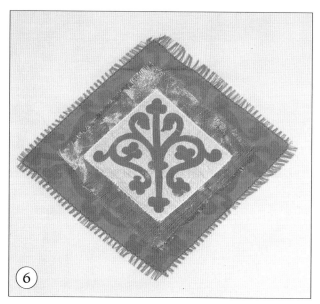

6. Position the squares centrally at the top of the muslin panels then pin them in place. Sew a line of zig-zag stitch around the largest square, and around the smallest square. Try to sew approximately 0.5cm (¼in) in from the edge.

7. Turn the fabric in twice to form a 1cm (⅜in) hem, and machine stitch all round. Iron the fabric to fix the paint. Cut eight 25cm (9in) lengths of ribbon for each panel. Fold the ribbon in half and hand sew to the top edge of the fabric panel. Use four pieces at the top and four pieces at the bottom of each panel. Tie the fabric to the screen.

OPPOSITE
Eastern clothes screen
This muslin screen and matching cushion are stamped with an abstract image. The stamping has been positioned to create a simple design. Appliquéd squares of contrasting muslin and opulent gold organza give the screen an exotic eastern flavour.

Ethnic throw

The beauty of this project lies in the random selection of stamped fabrics, colours and patterns. You can use up any oddments of plain fabrics you have to create a lively ethnic patchwork. If recycling fabrics, remember to wash, dry and iron them all before you start. Smooth, close-weave fabrics give the best results when stamping.

You will need

Heavy mustard fabric with uneven weave, 1.35 x 1.45m (4½ x 4¾ft)

Green open weave fabric, 0.3 x 1.5m (1 x 5ft)

Ticking, 0.3 x 1.5m (1 x 5ft)

Beige cotton, 0.3 x 1.5m (1 x 5ft)

Cream cotton, 0.3 x 1.5m (1 x 5ft)

Orange cotton, 0.3 x 1.5m (1 x 5ft)

Purple cotton, 0.3 x 1.5m (1 x 5ft)

Yellow cotton, 0.3 x 1.5m (1 x 5ft)

Mustard sewing thread

Decorative stamping paint: yellow, cream, brown, dark green, mid-green and terracotta

Decorative stamps: leaf, coil, zig-zag, lizard and bird

Applicator sponges and palette

Pinking shears

Scissors

Pins

Iron

Ruler and pencil

Small paintbrush

Note
Lay the heavy mustard fabric out before cutting. If it has an attractive selvedge, then do not try to trim or fray this. The selvedge will require no sewing.

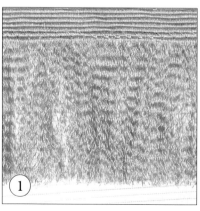

1. Pull out some of the weft threads from the edges of the heavy mustard fabric to create a 5cm (2in) frayed fringe. Sew a line of zig-zag stitch along the line where the fraying stops, to secure the edge.

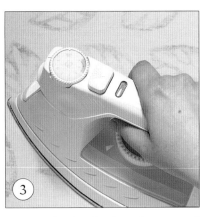

3. Iron the back of each piece of stamped fabric to fix the design. Adjust the setting on the iron to one that is suitable for the fabric you are ironing.

2. Stamp the cream, purple, yellow, beige and orange fabrics randomly all over using one or a selection of stamps and a colour of your choice. I have used paints to tone with the fabrics. As the fabric is quite thick, apply the paint with a small paintbrush rather than with an applicator sponge. Leave the paint to dry for at least twenty-four hours.

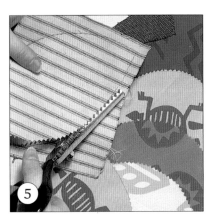

5. Cut leaf shapes out of some of the squares using pinking shears. Cut others down into smaller squares using the straight-edge scissors. Create a fringe around some of the small squares if you wish (see step 1).

4. Cut each piece of stamped fabric, the ticking and the green open weave fabric into 15cm (6in) squares.

6. Arrange the squares and leaves on top of each other. Try to be completely random and mix different colours and patterns. Sew the shapes together with a zig-zag stitch.

7. Lay the fabric squares on to the mustard backing fabric to create a border around the edge. I arranged some leaves within the border, and positioned four squares in the centre, but you can move the squares and leaves around until you are happy with the overall design. Pin to secure, and then sew in place.

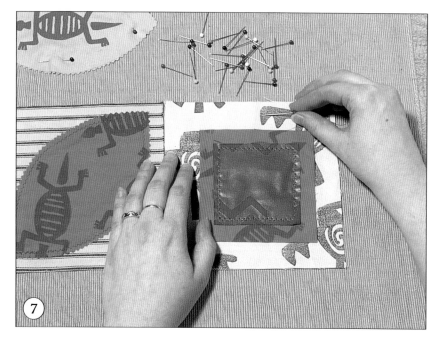

Ethnic throw
This colourful throw is made up of appliquéd patches of stamped fabrics which are assembled to give an African flavour. You can use this technique to style a matching picture and wall hanging.

CERAMICS, GLASS AND METAL

*Citrus cupboard • Terracotta pot • Mediterranean table
Primitive picture frame*

Very smooth non-porous surfaces can be quite difficult to stamp on as the paint has nothing to adhere to. It is worth spending time experimenting before undertaking any large project on an unusual surface. Three factors can affect the results achieved: the surface itself; the type of paint used; and the application technique.

Unglazed ceramics such as terracotta pots and biscuit-ware china present no real problems regarding paint application. However, glass, mirror, metal and glazed ceramics such as tiles and domestic china, have a completely non-porous surface and the stamping technique needs to vary slightly to allow for this. A stamp fully loaded with paint will tend to slide on the shiny surface. A specialist decorative stamping paint or an acrylic paint should be used and the minimum of paint should be applied to the stamp. To do this, load the stamp with paint, stamp on to a scrap piece of paper then, without reapplying paint, stamp on to your surface. When the paint is dry, apply several coats of tile varnish or clear acrylic car lacquer to seal the stamping.

Alternatively, you can purchase paints designed to work on specific surfaces: thermo-hardening ceramic paints fire in a domestic oven and specialist glass and mirror paints are also available. These paints all work with stamps but tend to give a very soft, pale, translucent colour. There are also primers now available which will prepare virtually any surface for painting or stamping. Always experiment first and follow the manufacturer's instructions with care.

A frosted decorative stamping effect can be worked on glass and mirror (see page 16) or the surfaces can be stamped with neat or diluted paint. Before you begin, the surface should be prepared by washing with soapy water to remove any grease. It should then be allowed to dry thoroughly. Both effects will withstand gentle washing, but are unsuitable for food containers or anything that requires regular washing. Protect the stamped images from chipping by applying several coats of clear acrylic car lacquer when dry.

Most sheet metal is supplied with a protective plastic film covering so no surface preparation is necessary, you simply need to remove the film. If your metal does not have this film, ensure the surface is free from dust and grease before you begin.

Citrus cupboard

Any small wooden cupboard is suitable to restyle for this project, but unfinished pine is ideal. The lemon stamped design and crisp, clean aluminium make this an ideal cupboard for a modern kitchen. Lemon emulsion paint is thinned with water to give a soft woodwash effect, so a small tester pot of paint should be sufficient to cover the piece. Try changing or painting the handles on an older cupboard to bring it up-to-date, or add a length of dowel for hanging utensils. You can alter the colour scheme and stamp to adapt this project for any room – woodwash with lime and stamp fish and shells for the bathroom, or stain the wood dark oak and stamp with classical flourishes for a grand dining room.

You will need

Wooden cupboard

Medium grade sandpaper

Damp cloth

0.5mm (0.020in) aluminium sheet

Large rounded nail

Small pointed nail

Hammer

Silicone glue

Emulsion paint: lemon

Decorative stamping paint: jade, dark green, yellow, orange, white, lemon and silver

Decorative stamps: lemons; lemon slices; and swirls

Sponge applicators and palette

1cm (½in) square piece of foam

Short length of dowel, or old thick marker pen

Solvent glue

Thin plywood (cut to fit the door panels)

Soft cloth

2.5cm (1in) masking tape

Cutting mat

Steel ruler

Scalpel

Old blanket or newspapers

Scrap paper

Sticky notelets

5 chrome-plated handles

1. Prepare the wooden surface in the same way as the writing slope (see step 1, page 22). Dilute the lemon emulsion paint using five parts water to one part paint. Apply a coat all over the cupboard. Leave to dry.

Note

If you are using an old cupboard, remove all paint or varnish using a paint stripper. Follow the manufacturer's instructions carefully. Sand thoroughly to remove any remaining paint. Wear a face mask to avoid inhaling paint or varnish dust.

2. Paint the plywood panels using dark green decorative stamping paint. Leave to dry. Mix a small amount of jade green to the dark green to make a slightly lighter green. Use this colour to stamp swirls all over the plywood panels.

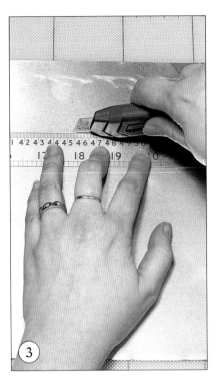

Note
You can use large old scissors to cut out the aluminium if you prefer. This will not, however, produce such a smooth line.

3. Cut two pieces of aluminium, each one to fit inside the door frame, allowing a 5cm (2in) gap all around. To do this, work on a cutting mat and use a steel ruler to get a straight edge. Make a series of small cuts, pressing lightly until you have created a deep groove, then bend the joint back and forth until the metal snaps.

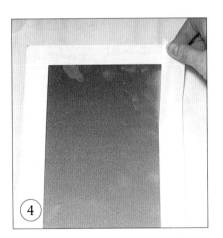

4. Use masking tape to mask all around the edge of both of the aluminium panels.

5. Apply dark green, jade, orange, yellow and lemon paint to your lemon stamp using a sponge applicator. Blend the colours (see page 12) then stamp on to both metal panels. As the aluminium is a very non-absorbent surface, stamp first on to scrap paper, and then on to the metal. Take care not to let the stamp slide on the metal.

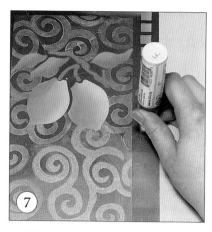

6. Mask the lemon (see page 27) on each panel. Apply silver paint to the swirls stamp and stamp all over both central areas. Leave to dry before removing the masking tape and the lemon mask.

7. Glue a 1cm (½in) square of foam on to the end of an old pen lid or a piece of dowel to make a small square stamp. Apply yellow and orange paint then stamp a border around each metal panel. Leave to dry.

8. Place one of the metal panels on a folded old blanket or a pile of newspaper. Use a hammer and a large rounded nail to punch dents into the metal. Hammer lightly to avoid punching straight through the metal. Use this technique to add a central vein to each leaf, and then scratch in smaller veins using the tip of a small pointed nail. Continue adding dents to create a border pattern around the panel. Repeat with the other metal panel.

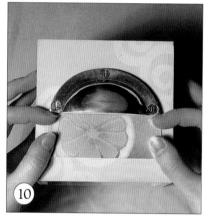

10. Stamp areas of the drawers using pale yellow and the swirls stamp. Leave to dry. Screw the handles in place. Decorate with small pieces of aluminium stamped using the lemon slice stamp. Glue them to the front of the drawers.

9. Use silicone glue to stick each metal panel centrally on to the plywood. Leave to set, then stick the pieces of plywood on to the doors of the cupboard.

Citrus cupboard

The stylish punched aluminium effect is easy to create and adds decorative detail to the stamped design. To finish this cupboard, I cut a piece of thick dowel the inside width of the cupboard, painted it dark green, then attached it to the cupboard using wardrobe rail fittings, to create extra storage. I also rubbed clear furniture wax into the finished piece to protect it. Matching kitchen accessories have been stamped, including a trompe l'oeil effect lemon tree which is made up of many stamped images and includes a hand-painted trunk and pot.

Terracotta pot

Jazz up terracotta pots with decorative stamping, ageing effects and lashings of colour. Choose your stamp carefully: a large stamp is easier to apply to a large pot than a small one. If your pot is very small, then stick to a small stamp or just decorate the rim. Foam-backed stamps are ideal as they will curve around the pot. If decorating an old pot, wash it first with a disinfectant and scrub gently to remove any mould growth. Do not worry about any small chips – these will add to the aged effect.

You will need
Terracotta pot

Decorative stamping paint: yellow, cream, pale turquoise, mid-green, jade, brown and gold

Old 4cm (1½in) paintbrush

Small paintbrush

Applicator sponge and palette

Decorative stamp: ivy

Rubber solution glue

Powdered filler

Sawdust or clean sand

Tinted antiquing wax

2 soft lint-free cloths

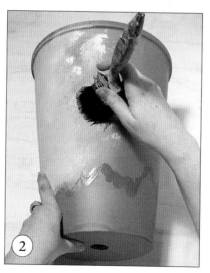

1. Paint a wiggly line of rubber solution glue approximately one fifth of the way up from the base of the pot. The more wiggly and jagged the line, the better.

2. Paint the section above the wiggly line using mid-green, pale turquoise, yellow and cream mixed on a 4cm (1½in) brush. Scrub the paint into the pot. Try to get subtle colour changes each time you reload the brush, and paint in random strokes. Leave to dry.

3. Mix up a paste using one part powdered filler, one part sawdust (or sand) and four parts water. Use the 4cm (1½in) paintbrush to apply this mixture to the lower section of the pot, under the glue line. Apply the paste in a stippling motion. Leave to dry.

4. Stipple a mixture of mid-green, pale turquoise, brown and gold paint roughly on to the filler to create a verdigris effect. Leave to dry.

5. Peel off the rubber solution glue. You can use your finger to rub off any stubborn patches.

6. Blend mid-green and jade paint on an ivy stamp (see page 12). Press one end of the stamp on to the pot then carefully press along its length, taking care not to shift the image. Stamp around the top of the pot.

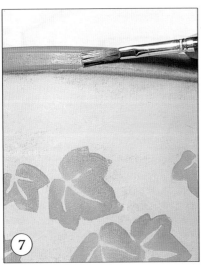

7. Paint a solid line of mid-green around the rim of the pot using a small paintbrush. Leave to dry.

8. Use a lint-free cloth to rub tinted antiquing wax all over the finished pot. Make sure you apply plenty of wax, and try to leave an uneven finish. Leave to dry for a few moments, then buff up with a clean lint-free cloth.

Note
If you find that you have a gap left around the pot that is not big enough for the whole ivy stamp, wash the stamp then apply paint to only one or two leaves to fill the space.

Note
You can make your own tinted wax by mixing a small amount of burnt sienna or raw umber oil paint with clear soft furniture wax. Wax can be corrosive, so any surplus mixture should be stored in a metal or glass container.

Terracotta pots

These pots are transformed using sun-drenched colours and they will brighten up any corner of your garden. A well-chosen stamp will make light work of decorating even a difficult curved surface. A layer of tinted wax will help protect your pot from the elements, but you may need to move the pot in winter as frost can be very damaging.

Mediterranean table

This unusual project uses an old table that is resurfaced to allow stamped tiles to be inset. To do this, simply lay your tiles on the old table top to create a border. Use matchsticks or pieces of thick card to space the tiles for grouting. Measure the rectangle in the centre and the border surrounding the tiles. Cut timber to these dimensions (a good DIY store will do this for you), remembering to use timber slightly thicker than your chosen tiles to allow for the adhesive beneath them. Alternatively, you could replace the tiles on a junk shop find.

Tile varnish will protect the stamped images, and make the table durable. Alternatively, use clear acrylic car lacquer.

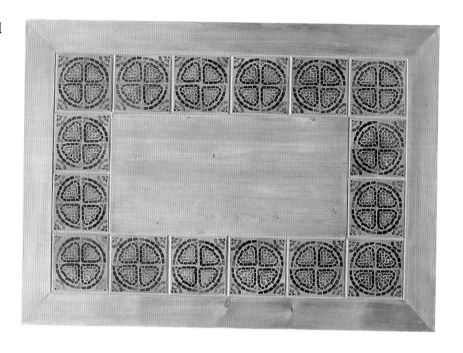

You will need
Old table
Terracotta quarry tiles
Plywood
Acrylic decorative stamping paint: cream, red, yellow, mid-green, gold and brown
Decorative stamp: mosaic design
Clear air-drying tile varnish
6.5cm (2½in) old paintbrush
Applicator sponges and palette
Tile adhesive
Strong epoxy glue
Matchsticks
Grout
Grout spreader
Damp cloth

1. Decant pools of cream, brown, green and yellow paint onto a palette. Mix two parts paint to one part water. Blend together on the brush then apply this colourwash to each of the tiles. Leave to dry.

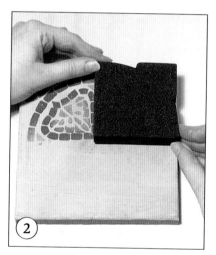

2. Use an applicator sponge to apply brown, red, yellow, mid-green and gold paint to the mosaic stamp. Blend the colours to soften the effect (see page 12). Stamp in all four corners of the tile. Leave to dry.

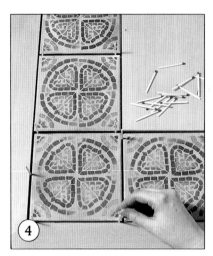

3. Stipple all over the tiles using air-drying tile varnish. Leave to dry for at least forty-eight hours. Repeat, then leave to dry again.

4. Spread tile adhesive into the area to be filled with tiles, then position the tiles using matchsticks or pieces of thick card for spacing. Leave to dry, following the manufacturer's instructions. Remove the spacers.

5. Follow the manufacturer's instructions to apply grout in between the tiles. Use a grout spreader to do this, and wipe the grout away from the edges of the tiles using a damp cloth.

Mediterranean table
Stamping is a quick and easy way to achieve an authentic-looking Mediterranean mosaic design. This table top has been transformed using painted and stamped terracotta tiles, and a wooden surround.

Primitive picture frame

Create three-dimensional stamped images by pressing a stamp into soft clay. Practice first, in order to gauge how hard you need to press to achieve a well-defined image. Air-hardening clay is the easiest to use but this may take up to forty-eight hours to dry, so check the manufacturer's instructions carefully before you start and allow yourself enough time to complete the project. This technique is also possible using fine papier mâché, oven-hardening clay or, if you have access to a kiln, regular clay.

You will need a piece of MDF for the backing of the frame and a piece of glass, cut and ground to the same size as your mount, to finish. Most good DIY stores will cut MDF, and you can ask your local framer or glass merchant to prepare the glass for you.

You will need
250g (½lb) air-hardening clay
Plain white paper
Old 4cm (1½in) brush
Decorative stamping paint: cream, brown, yellow and white
Decorative stamp: swirls
Applicator sponges and palette
Pale gold and copper gilding wax
MDF, 14cm (5½in) square, with a 9cm (3½in) square aperture
Glass, 8.5cm (3¼in) square
2 pieces of mount board, 8.5cm (3¼in) square
Photograph or picture
Ruler
Craft knife
Lint-free soft cloth
Glue and glue gun
25cm (10in) thin gold cord
Two lengths of scrap wood, approximately 1.5cm (½in) thick
Rolling pin
2.5cm (1in) masking tape

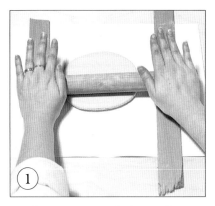

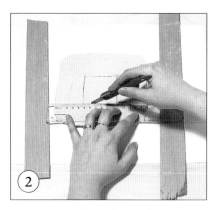

1. Place a piece of plain white paper on your work surface. Kneed the air-hardening clay until it is soft and smooth. Lay one length of scrap wood either side of the clay, then roll out the clay with a rolling pin. Use the pieces of wood as runners, to ensure that the clay has an even thickness all over.

2. Use your hands to shape a 16cm (6¼in) square. Measure in 5cm (2in) from all sides and then mark out a 6cm (2¼in) square in the middle. Use a ruler and a craft knife to cut out this aperture.

3. Position the swirls stamp over the clay, then press down firmly and evenly to leave an indentation. Repeat all over the frame. Do not allow the images to overlap. Leave to dry for at least forty-eight hours.

4. Load an old 4cm (1½in) paintbrush with dots of cream, brown, yellow and white paint. Dab the brush on to the side of the palette to mix the colours roughly. Stipple the paint all over the frame by dabbing the brush up and down. Try to get the paint down into the grooves. Leave to dry.

5. Use your finger to rub pale gold gilding wax into the raised pattern on the frame. Use the same technique and copper gilding wax to add highlights to other areas. Leave to dry for approximately five minutes before buffing up with a lint-free soft cloth.

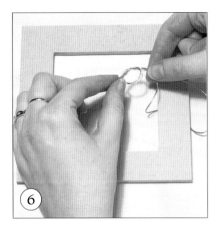

6. Tie a piece of gold cord around the top of the MDF. Position the knot centrally.

7. Use a glue gun to apply glue to the back of the frame.

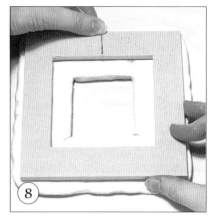

8. Sandwich the knot between the MDF and the back of the frame. Hold in place for a few moments while the glue sets.

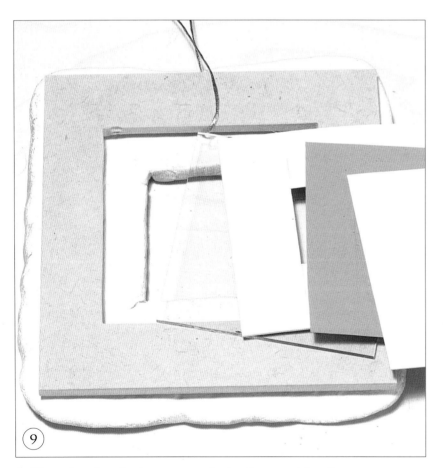

9. Place the glass in the aperture hole, then position the mount board. Now add a photograph or picture of your choice, and finally place another piece of mount board on top.

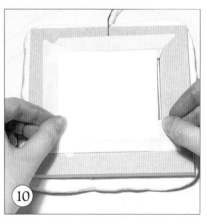

10. Tape the final piece of mount board securely in position using 2.5cm (1in) masking tape.

Primitive picture frame

Stamping in clay adds an exciting dimension, giving deep embossed effects. Gold and copper gilding wax are used to highlight the raised design, which adds a warm sumptuous glimmer. Adapt this technique to make subtle baroque-style mirrors, wall plaques, even decorated matching plates or bottles as shown here.

INDEX